T0115177

Journey to the Heart
OF FORGIVENESS

Journey to the Heart
OF FORGIVENESS

MO BRADY

BALBOA.
PRESS

A DIVISION OF HAY HOUSE

ISBN: 978-1-4525-5546-1 (sc)
ISBN: 978-1-4525-5547-8 (e)
Library of Congress Control Number: 2012913127

Balboa Press books may be ordered through booksellers or by contacting:

Balboa Press
A Division of Hay House
1663 Liberty Drive
Bloomington, IN 47403
www.balboapress.com
1-(877) 407-4847

Because of the dynamic nature of the Internet, any web addresses or
links contained in this book may have changed since publication and
may no longer be valid. The views expressed in this work are solely those
of the author and do not necessarily reflect the views of the publisher,
and the publisher hereby disclaims any responsibility for them.

The author of this book does not dispense medical advice or prescribe the use
of any technique as a form of treatment for physical, emotional, or medical
problems without the advice of a physician, either directly or indirectly. The
intent of the author is only to offer information of a general nature to help
you in your quest for emotional and spiritual well-being. In the event you use
any of the information in this book for yourself, which is your constitutional
right, the author and the publisher assume no responsibility for your actions.

Any people depicted in stock imagery provided by Thinkstock are
models, and such images are being used for illustrative purposes only.
Certain stock imagery © Thinkstock.

Printed in the United States of America
Balboa Press rev. date: 07/23/2012

Dedicated with love to
My Dad, who taught me to be resilient
in the face of challenge,
My Mom, who taught me to be true
to myself in all ways,
My two children, Lindsey and David,
who are my
joy and inspiration,
And
My husband and best friend, Jim,
Who passed away in March of 2011.
He was a lifelong source of support
And tenderness.

Contents

Preface.. xi

Surrender 1

Inner Magic 11

Earth's Breath 15

Glacial Falls 21

Bliss 26

Sonoran Twilight. 37

The Gem. 43

Nimbus 48

Grace. 51

Unfolding 60

Awakening the Divine Within

In an open meadow warmed by the sun
and embraced by a circle of swaying trees
tender flowers bloom.

As their roots reach deep and soak in
nourishment from the Earth
each new flower lifts its face to receive
the warm loving light.

Soft breezes carry the seeds from each bloom
to new parts of the meadow where they
nestle in the soil to gain strength
for their own future Awakening.

As each of us remembers how to reside
deep within our divine essence
allowing us to connect directly
to the source of our Wisdom
the meadow will be awash in flowers.

Collectively,
we are the sun,
the trees,
the meadow,
the flowers,
the soil and
the breeze.

Preface

I wrote the poem "Awakening the Divine Within" many years ago to express my inner knowing about the vast healing potential within us. Each one of us is a spiritual being connected to the Loving Source and by going within ourselves can activate all the healing energy necessary to express our true potential. We have each chosen to be here on the planet at this particular moment of human evolution for a reason. By journeying within ourselves and connecting to the reservoir of wisdom that resides there we can heal whatever emotional wounds block the fulfillment of our life purpose. As we each begin to live directly from that deep heart space, our joy and peace will inspire others to heal themselves as well.

Surrender

The box of memories held secrets
Wrapped in anger, shame and guilt,
But once the lid was sprung
And light allowed inside
What emerged
Was a precious treasure

G lancing out the kitchen window to the backyard I caught sight of their little blond heads, playing some imaginary game with my own two small children, completely unaware of what the day would hold for them. My two little blond nephews had spent a lot of time at our house that year as their mom, Valerie, had been battling ovarian cancer. As I watched them contentedly at play, I grabbed a tissue to wipe away my own tears. Valerie had gone into the hospital three weeks earlier and the boys were expecting her to come home soon. A few hours later I received the call I had been dreading, that Valerie had passed away. Hiding my own grief I tried to act as normal as possible, so that my brother could deliver the news to his sons himself. Valerie was only 33, and I was consumed with sadness at the thought of her two small boys, ages 5 and 8, navigating life without her tender care.

It had been an emotional roller coaster ride of a year, first with Valerie's diagnosis, then through long months of grueling chemotherapy. The prognosis from blood work at the end of chemotherapy was bright. We celebrated with a big family party. A month later when they did a "second look" surgery to make sure things inside looked good they found the cancer had actually metastasized to her liver and there was nothing more they could do. Most of my energy that year had been devoted to supporting my brother and his family as they battled this illness together. When Valerie died it felt as if I fell off an emotional cliff.

My grief over Valerie's passing tore open a deep wound inside me. I developed an intense case of insomnia, and could not sleep through the night for about six months, despite using prescription sleeping medications. I remember lying down on my pillow one night desperately wondering if I would ever be able to sleep through the night again. At the time I could not imagine it would ever be possible, and I felt so completely at the end of my emotional rope. It seemed like sanity was on top of a cliff and I was hanging over the abyss clinging to the edge with my fingernails, frantically trying to pull myself back up to safety. I am not someone who operates well on lack of sleep, as my family can surely attest to! I became extremely irritable and emotional, yelling at my children and my husband at the slightest provocation. I found it difficult to go anywhere where I had to interact with others. As this dragged on for months, something inside me knew that this deep emotional chasm I had fallen into involved more that just Valerie's death.

In retrospect I see the incredible gift that Valerie gave me with her passing. I felt so completely on the verge of losing my sanity that I surrendered to a whisper of wisdom within me. It was as if the grief I experienced from her death cracked open a source within me that I had been keeping a tight lid on for a very long time.

During this tumultuous time I was at my daughter's softball practice one afternoon, and a friend of mine told me she had picked up a new book. She hadn't read it, but thought I might be interested in it. The book was *Anatomy of the Spirit* by Caroline Myss. That book was just the key I needed to unlock the door to myself. With exquisite compassion and clarity, Caroline outlines the energy connections between our body, mind and spirit, and how blocking our connection to our emotional and spiritual self can manifest as illness in our physical self. Her words made so much sense to me, and the personal stories she used to illustrate her concepts gave me hope. I soaked up the book like a sponge and looked for clues to connect to my inner self so that my story could be revealed. My motivation was that I desperately wanted to begin sleeping again. Using her book like a compass I began to look inside myself for answers to regain my sense of wholeness.

In *Anatomy of the Spirit* Caroline creates a beautiful tapestry, weaving together the emotional, physical and spiritual aspects of the seven Christian sacraments, the Kabbalah Tree of Life and the Hindu chakras. Her writings resonated deeply with me and I began a practice of meditation with an earnest intention to heal myself emotionally, physically and spiritually. One of her insights centers around the idea that our physical self is an outward manifestation of what is occurring for us on an emotional and spiritual level. I began to ask myself, "What physical issues is my body currently displaying that would give me a clue as to where I need to begin my healing?" The one thing that came to mind

3

immediately was that I had been suffering for years from bleeding hemorrhoids and despite numerous trips to the doctors, had little relief from them. In her book, hemorrhoids are linked to repressed anger and the first chakra, which deals with security and family of origin issues. At first, I was a little at a loss what to do with this information. Raised Catholic, and attending Catholic schools until 8th grade, I was taught that it was not acceptable to display anger as a "good Catholic girl". I began trying to meditate as Caroline suggested in the book. I decided to ask myself before I meditated what I possibly had to be angry about. To my great surprise, I received the answer one morning very clearly. It was as if I had given my inner child permission to reveal something that I was not consciously aware of. I received the sudden insight that I was angry with my parents. I opened my eyes from my meditative state almost in shock, and asked myself, "What would I possibly have to be angry with my parents about?" As quickly as I asked the answer came to me. I was angry with them for emotionally abandoning me when I was 18 and became pregnant my freshman year in college. I sat there on the carpet in my bedroom as this insight sank in. I had not been consciously aware of my anger. My parents were wonderful people and I felt guilty for having those feelings. Accepting that maybe this was something I needed to acknowledge and heal led me to invest myself in going back and revisiting the emotions of that time in my life.

I had been a straight "A" student, graduating as valedictorian from my high school class. Now a freshman in college, I had been dating someone for about six months and feeling very in love. The very first time we had sex, I became pregnant. I talked myself out of it for months. How could I possibly be unlucky enough to get pregnant after having sex one time! After two missed periods, I finally went to a clinic and took a pregnancy test and it was positive! As a young Catholic woman very connected to her church, the idea of an abortion was completely out of the question for me. Counseling us against getting married, my parents felt that the best course of action was for me to have the baby in secret and then return to my life as if nothing had happened. Truly my boyfriend and I were not prepared for marriage and children at the time, so I agreed.

Because of our closeness to the Catholic Church, my parents arranged through Catholic Social Services for me to move to another city two hours away. I was to live with a family with two small children, and serve as their nanny and housekeeper in exchange for my stay. I was not allowed to tell anyone where I was going, except for my two sisters, Kathy and Eileen. My three younger brothers were not even aware of where I was going or why. Instead, we came up with the story that I had suddenly decided to drop out of college and had gone to stay with relatives in another state to take a break. Stuffing all my own feelings, I lied to everyone I knew, even my closest friends.

The family I stayed with was very welcoming, and had assisted other young women in the same way, but I still felt completely emotionally severed from everyone I knew and loved. This feeling was compounded by the fact that I felt I was hiding a big, shameful secret. Catholic Social Services provided free counseling, but most of the sessions I spent there just left me feeling worse and worse about myself. To attend these counseling sessions I had to travel on a city bus, which passed right by a large university that many of my friends were attending. I held my breath every time, scared to death that one of them would board the bus and discover my secret, as there was no hiding the fact that I was very pregnant. Whether it was true or not, I felt like I was being looked down upon and judged everywhere I went for being young, unmarried and pregnant. These days that stigma has somewhat disappeared, but back in the mid 1970's it was alive and well.

My parents would call and visit, but their busy lives were full with commitments to their other five children still at home. My boyfriend would also call and visit, but in my absence he began to date someone else, explaining to me that it was because he missed me so much. Gradually, the emotional support he offered me evaporated, as he became more and more involved with his new girlfriend. By the time our son was born, he was deep into an emotional commitment with someone else. He did not want to stop dating her when I returned home, so our relationship ended.

Catholic Social Services also provided access to a physician to whom we paid a minimal fee to provide prenatal care and deliver the baby. I was very dedicated to eating well and taking good care of myself during the pregnancy so that my baby would be as healthy as possible. The family I lived with assisted me in connecting with a birthing coach who taught me breathing and relaxation techniques for the delivery. She was going to be present at the delivery with me.

As luck would have it, the baby arrived late and my birthing coach was away on a trip, so she was not able to assist me. I was totally unprepared for the actual pain involved in childbirth. The only thing I can really recall from the birth was screaming at the top of my lungs as the physician pulled my son out with forceps without giving me adequate pain medication. I felt a crack, as if my body was actually being split in half. Between that and the very long episiotomy I received to repair my tearing, I had the definite feeling that this Catholic doctor was somehow trying to "teach me a lesson".

My 9 lb. 4 oz. baby boy was beautiful and absolutely radiant! I held him once to say good-bye and prayed that his life would be blessed with his new family. I knew in my heart that I was giving the most sacred gift possible, and I released him with love.

All of this was before the days of cell phones and facebook accounts, so it was relatively easy to fall off the face of the planet and then suddenly reappear seven months later. A week after my son was born, I returned from my "relaxing trip to visit relatives". Outwardly I may have looked like the same person when I returned to Phoenix, but inwardly I was an emotional basket case. I could not even sit upright in the car during the two hour ride home from Tucson, as my episiotomy was still so sore. As I struggled to find my emotional balance, my survival instincts kicked in to protect the gaping hole in my wounded psyche. I did the only thing I knew how to do, which was to stuff all of the pain deep inside myself to a place where I hoped I would never have to revisit it. I sealed off a part of myself, because to feel the loss was so intense, I could not cope unless I buried it. There were times over the next several years that the emotional pain would suddenly rush to the surface when I would see a tiny baby. Unable to stop the tears, I would race into the nearest bathroom to hide in a stall and sob. These episodes just made me summon up more inner resolve to bury the pain deeper still, so that nothing would bring it to the surface. I prayed that my son would understand that I would never be able to contact him in the future, because I felt that if I ever fully revisited the painful memories, their power would kill me. Little did I know that to shut off a part of myself was to cause damage to my entire being. I did my best to fall back into my previous life as a high-performing student. I followed my love of art, and graduated from college with a Bachelor of Fine Arts degree.

Now here I sat on the carpet in my bedroom trying to come to terms with the idea that the key to my feeling better might be in revisiting this painful experience and forgiving my parents for how they had handled the situation. I was scared to death to unearth feelings that I had kept buried for twenty years, however the recent loss of my sister-in-law had stripped me bare. I no longer had the energy necessary to keep all of this past pain buried. My inner turbulence had reached critical mass and now in order to heal, I needed to reach deep inside and allow this old wound to completely rise to the surface in order to be acknowledged, healed and released.

Beginning with the ideas in Caroline's book, I began to meditate with the intention of understanding what religious and social conditions might have made my parents react the way they did twenty years ago. As I slowly detached from the idea of them as my "mom and dad" I tried to embrace what it must have been like in their shoes as Catholic parents in the mid 1970's. The more I opened my heart in meditation the easier it became, and I began to accept that they were truly only doing what they thought was best for me in that circumstance. They had not consciously set out to hurt me, and did not have the capacity at that time to realize the deep emotional impact the experience had on me. I tried to meditate once a day, but as the process unfolded over several months I began to receive insights at other times of day as well, even when I wasn't meditating. My inner intuitive voice became stronger and more present as I consciously set my intention to forgive. Something inside me was beginning to soften and melt and I gradually began to sleep through the night again.

This journey of forgiveness was reconnecting me to my inner self. I was learning as if for the first time in my life to truly listen and trust my inner voice. I was also realizing how much spiritual support I was being given. I felt guided by grace not only to forgive, but also to recognize and release all of the personal shame and guilt I had chosen to heap upon myself from the experience. I cultivated my inner voice and consciously gave it permission to access whatever it needed to reveal to me so that I could feel whole again. In the process I realized that I had been carrying quite a load of negative feelings about my own self worth.

When I was growing up my family was a big fan of the Carol Burnette Show. We sat perched around the family room watching her crazy antics as she portrayed so many different eccentric characters. It was one of my favorite times to share with my Dad because Tim Conway and Harvey Korman's routines elicited such belly laughs from him that his eyes would well up with tears of joy. As the years passed and life became so complicated and heavy feeling, I treasured those memories in my mind's eye. Not only did they remind me of the joy of my youth, but I drew upon those eccentric characters and Carol's ability to examine the very ordinary in life and bring humor to it. As I began to travel down the path of forgiveness, the mental visual that kept occurring to me was like a skit from the Carol Burnette Show: an oddly dressed woman is grunting and groaning as she pushes a

9

shopping cart, which is overflowing with packages. Some of those packages might be labeled guilt, shame, bitterness, or anger. Angels are walking by, and one by one try to lift a package from her cart to lighten her load. The character is so accustomed to pushing her load that she sees their gestures as intrusive, and swats them away wildly with an old broken umbrella. How dare they mess with her stuff!! I imagined myself as that character and made a commitment to empty my cart and lighten my load. I would call the visual to mind whenever my emotional buttons would get pushed and ask, "What am I still carting around that I could release and lighten my load?" Just consciously setting the intention was enough to set in motion a wonderful healing journey.

Inner Magic

Trickling,
Bubbling,
Bursting,
Flowing with abundance,
The universal river of love
Carries us along
With its magic

I n her book *Anatomy of the Spirit*, Caroline Myss talks in detail about the path of forgiveness and gives examples of how to proceed. I practiced many of her ideas and worked through the issue of forgiving my parents. I could see the injured parts of their lives and how their personal experiences led them to feel that how they handled my pregnancy was in my best interest. Shortly after I had worked through forgiving my parents, one of my younger brothers came into town for a visit. He and I took my two children to a baseball game. At the baseball game, about 15 rows down and 10 seats over sat the boyfriend that I had shared the pregnancy experience with. I had not seen him for over 20 years, but I was sure that it was him. He and his friends left the game early, so I never spoke to him. I had begun paying attention to coincidences in life, realizing that they could be gifts from Spirit. I knew that I must have seen him for a reason. After putting my children to bed that evening, I sat down to meditate, and asked for Spirit to reveal why I had seen him. The answer came, "You need to forgive him too." Again, I was not even consciously aware that I was angry with him. I sat in silence, allowing the feelings to rise to the surface. I realized that I felt that I had been the only one that bore the consequences of our having sex, and was also angry with him for emotionally abandoning me. I can't honestly say that I was very excited about the prospect of having to forgive him too. In fact I felt like a two-year-old bargaining with Spirit, "Don't you think I've already grown enough? Do I really have to do this too?" Once I got over my own childlike protests, I opened myself to the forgiveness process, knowing it would only free me further from the pain I had held onto for so long.

For most of my adult life I had thought of the idea of forgiveness as letting someone else off the hook for the pain they caused you. I was beginning to understand forgiveness in an entirely new way. Each person that causes us pain is also just a wounded soul, doing the best they can at that particular moment in time. They have their own emotional wounds that motivate their actions. Seeing others in this tender way allows us to better understand the source of their actions. The forgiveness seems to flow naturally, when we truly take the time and open our heart to see the other from a soul perspective. The flip side of this is that we can choose not to feel hurt by someone's actions if we realize we actually have that choice before the pain occurs. We are all just acting and reacting based on our own inner wounds. When I was 18, my parent's opinion of me was extremely important, and

I chose to feel shamed by their sending me away. At that time, I did not have the self-awareness to maintain my own self-esteem through that difficult experience.

About a year had passed since I first began reading *Anatomy of the Spirit*. Wow, what a year that was! I felt like I had retrieved a part of myself that had been lost for two decades. I had reconnected to my inner voice with the knowing that we are not traveling this life alone. We truly have help from an infinite, Loving Source. I wrote the poem at the beginning of this chapter to express my gratitude for the love I felt was guiding me. I used the metaphor of a river, because it was only when I surrendered to its fluid energy that my heart began to heal.

I continued to meditate on a regular basis and my mind grew more calm and quiet. It was easier to hear the guidance of my inner voice and I practiced making the connection stronger. I began going to my local library and listening to inspirational books on tape. The first one I was drawn to was Wayne Dyer's *The Awakened Life*. I listened to it in my car everywhere I drove, and allowed his concepts to sink in. There was also a conversation on tape between Wayne Dyer and Deepak Chopra called *Living Beyond Miracles*. Each time I listened, some new bit of wisdom would penetrate my thoughts. One especially potent idea that I decided to experiment with was the notion of actively creating our own reality by focusing on the "feeling" of what we wanted to experience. The idea was to imagine what it would physically feel like in our body to have the desired experience, and then go into the field of infinite possibilities, release the intention, and let Spirit handle the details. Deepak described the field of infinite possibilities as being the gap between our thoughts. It was the silence beyond space and time where all possibilities existed as pure potential. By getting out of the way and not trying to control the flow of events, we allow the universe to orchestrate events in whatever way is in the highest good of all involved to bring the desired experience.

I carried this idea into my meditation practice and would actively imagine the "feelings" I wanted to create within my close personal relationships, especially with my husband, Jim, and my children, Lindsey and David. I just imagined how it would feel inside my belly if I could be experiencing exactly the kind of playful, intimate relationships I desired. I set photographs of Jim and my kids on my bathroom counter to remind myself daily to maintain the vision of the optimal relationship experiences I wanted to create.

Earth's Breath

Playful,
Soothing,
Invigorating,
The elusive wind
Dances with all beings
As she beckons them
To awaken
To the rhythms
Of the cosmos

As I was creating new openings in my life, I reflected on the concept of following my passion. Both Wayne Dyer and Deepak Chopra spoke about how the soul draws us towards our life's purpose by igniting our passion. I had never had any interest in poetry, but began reading some of the spiritual poetry of Rumi, the poet I heard Deepak quote most often. On one of Deepak's CDs he quoted the poetry of Rumi and Tagore. The poems spoke of a passion for being alive on this earth. At the time I was working part-time for a local art gallery. In the evening, after my children were in bed I started making beaded earrings as a creative outlet. What began with making earrings for myself soon grew into making gifts for friends. Late one night as I was beading and listening to Deepak reading poetry I had a sudden insight that the passionate feeling he described was exactly how I felt when I was involved in any artistic pursuit. Immersing myself in creating beauty always carried me to a timeless place where I felt wrapped in joy. I decided that night to pursue making beaded jewelry as a business.

In choosing a name for my new company, I wanted it to reflect the new person I was becoming. I settled on the name "Luminous Beads" to reflect my desire to radiate loving energy to everyone I came in contact with. I am lucky enough to be married to a very gifted illustrator who taught me how to use Photoshop software on the computer to design my own logo. I created a symbol to convey playful radiating love. My business began by word of mouth and I started making earrings and selling them to friends. In turn, my friends would give me new ideas of other jewelry items they wanted me to make for them. Soon I was making bracelets, necklaces and anklets. My passion for creating has always been ignited by color, and I found I had a gift for combining unusual colors in my pieces. Whenever I have focused myself on a creative endeavor I find that inspiration presents itself everywhere. I began to use these color inspirations to name my pieces, such as "Desert Dawn" for the sage greens, purples and golds that the early morning light brings to a desert landscape. Eventually I branched out to do local art shows and jewelry parties, and my husband designed a website for me.

My jewelry business presented new opportunities to facilitate my inner healing. At first I was rather surprised that anyone was interested enough to buy my earrings or bracelets. As

I continued to meditate and observed these thoughts, I realized that I did not have a very strong sense of self worth, and it was being reflected in my low expectations about my jewelry. I noticed that I had a difficult time asking for money for things I made. With this new insight about myself I choose to consciously work to improve in that area. I monitored my thoughts and noticed that I worried a great deal about nearly everything in life. Finding it difficult to simply shut off these thoughts, I decided to give my mind another task to occupy itself. I thought of my negative thoughts like a two-year-old who is playing with an object that isn't safe for them. If you try to force the object out of their hands, a struggle will break out. Instead you need to cajole them with an object they find more engaging. Growing up Catholic, there were many prayers I knew by heart, and one of my favorites had been the Hail Mary. I set a conscious intention that whenever I found my mind had slipped into worry or negative thinking, I would redirect it by giving it the Hail Mary to recite. I would actually find myself saying, "Sorry little missie, but we're not going there anymore.....Hail Mary full of grace, the Lord is with you....." It worked surprisingly well, as I knew that prayer so well that I could slip into it easily and set my mind on its new task with little effort. The more aware I became of observing my thought habits, the less negative they became. When the old worry habit tried to show up, I redirected with the Hail Mary. At times, it really felt like a game with a two-year-old and I began to find humor in the way my mind was so accustomed to falling into the worry groove. It was like a well-worn skip on a record and I had to consciously be the hand that lifted the needle from the groove to allow the music to play again.

The jewelry business began with a small amount of money and I bought very inexpensive glass and cast pewter beads, relying on my sense of design to produce unusual combinations. I drew upon my work experience from my early twenties when I worked in New York designing for a knitwear and clothing importer. I remembered how we figured out costs for an item and used portions of the profits to reinvest in growing the company. I created a series of bracelets that could be easily duplicated to cut down on the individual designing time. For each sale I made, I would set aside a portion of the money to purchase new materials. Without having much capital to begin with, I was able to slowly grow my business this way. Branching out to more expensive materials, I ventured into natural gemstones and sterling silver. I came across beading books that talked about the healing energy of gemstones and began to create pieces with healing themes. When my kids were at school I would sometimes string beads all day, falling into a very relaxed meditative rhythm. I focused on breathing very deep and regular to allow myself to settle into the creative moment. Inspired by the colors and gemstones, short poems would form in my thoughts to describe the healing energy of a particular piece and I began writing poetry to go with my jewelry. The poetry became another aspect of my business and I noticed that my customers were sometimes just as attracted to the poetry as they were to the jewelry. I created small cards with the poetry to accompany the jewelry. One of my most popular pieces was a bracelet called "Earth and Sky" that I kept as part of my line for several years. It was a combination of turquoise, copper, picture jasper and clear glass beads. This was the poem that accompanied it:

Earth and Sky

As the Earth nurtures
Our physical being
the
Eternal Loving Spirit
Caresses our Soul

The art shows I participated in for my jewelry business involved long weekend days away from home. My kids were still young and we missed spending time with each other on those weekends. When possible they would come spend part of the day at the show with me. In doing so they became active participants in the business, to the point where they wanted to create their own items to sell. Seeing it as an opportunity to empower them, I encouraged them each to design their own logo, and they each sold earrings that they chose the beads for. Lindsey was about 11 at the time, and David was 7. Their playful logos reflected their ages and personalities wonderfully. Lindsey used the name Kid's Kolors. Her hand drawn letterforms were each a different color and style, full of squiggles and spirals. David called his Kid's Fun and drew a bright round yellow smiley face, complete with a mouth full of teeth and spiked hair! You could not help but smile at their logos, and my customers loved talking with them and purchasing their creations.

In the early days of my jewelry business there were not many bead stores in Phoenix, and I used to drive north to a small shop near Prescott, Arizona that sold an eclectic variety of things, including beads. It was a rustic old building, packed with handmade Native American items, masks from Africa, pottery from Peru, antiques of all sorts and a very unique collection of beads. Part of what I enjoyed about the trip was the drive through the beautiful Arizona terrain of desert and mountains. There is nothing quite like the expansive horizons that Arizona offers. My spirit was nourished on these drives as I soaked in the beauty of the landscape. One time I was taking the drive and David decided to accompany me. I figured we would enjoy our time together and he would probably enjoy looking around at all the fascinating items in the shop while I did my bead shopping. Little did I know how much he would enjoy the place! He was captivated by a selection of small animal skulls that were in a glass case and convinced me to buy him one. I happen to love the artist Georgia O'Keefe and could easily understand the beauty he saw in those dry bones. David had begun to watercolor a bit at the encouragement of my husband, and the skulls became one of his subjects. He saved up his money and made the trip another time with me to purchase several more skulls, which he carefully labeled once we got home.

On one of these drives, David and I stopped at the Sunset Point rest area, in between Phoenix and Prescott. Sunset Point is located on a high plateau facing a beautiful grouping of mountains with a deep valley in between. The concrete terraces of the rest area are perched at the edge of the plateau where visitors can gaze across the valley at the mountains. As David and I stood on the terrace I explained to him how I enjoyed standing there, breathing in deeply and imagining myself soaring over the valley to the top of the mountains on the other side. I encouraged him to try it, as it always seemed to open up my awareness. After we stood there for a few minutes, he looked up at me and said, "I have a name for a new bracelet for you, "Valley Below." Shortly after that I designed a beautiful green aventurine bracelet, which reflected the energy of opening our heart centers and used the name he had given me that day.

Glacial Falls

As old doubts melt away
A crystal clear stream
Begins to cascade within us,
Cleansing
And Reawakening
Every fiber of our being

My jewelry business flourished for years and brought wonderful opportunities for friendships and personal growth. I crossed paths with so many other creative women at art shows. During slow times at weekend long shows we would visit with each other and share life experiences. I would often be carrying one of my favorite books by Caroline Myss or Deepak Chopra and our conversations would go to a deeper level about personal growth and healing. I realized that everyone has a story and is searching for ways to heal and connect to more joy in life. I would find myself giving away my favorite books to assist someone else on their path. During one particularly quiet weekend show I had brought along a book by a new author I had been drawn to, Judith Orloff. I had recently begun reading her book *Guide to Intuitive Healing*. Business was so slow that weekend that I was able to read over half the book, and her words really spoke to my heart. Her descriptions of highly empathic people fit me to the tee! She provided very concrete ideas on how to remain open and compassionate without absorbing everyone's pain, which is what I had been doing before. Even as a child I could just stand next to someone and palpably feel their joy, sadness or anger inside me. I realized that I had somehow developed the belief that to love other people I needed to absorb their pain myself, and as a consequence often felt down and fatigued. She gave many specific ways to shift this thinking and the quiet space of time at the art fair gave me time to absorb her ideas. Her words gave me tools to further transform my life and create healthy boundaries that honored my empathic nature.

I began journaling to remind myself of the new behaviors I wanted to incorporate to create a more balanced life with healthier boundaries and visualized myself saying and doing new things. I realized that just as I had felt abandoned by others at times in my life, I also abandoned my true self by not having healthy boundaries. In order for my natural empathy to be a useful tool for myself and others, I needed to use it more wisely. It always seemed that when I set an intention to shift a particular action or belief, Spirit would provide abundant opportunities to practice the new desired behavior. Humor was my constant companion, as I figured that the gig was that if we didn't get frequent chances to practice the behaviors we are shifting, we also miss out on the positive feedback to ourselves on how much we have grown. I seemed to attract more and more experiences to stand up for myself and with practice it became easier and easier to do so. I made a promise to myself that I was not going to give until it "hurt", like I had done in the past, but instead consider my feelings as part of the equation. I would not say, "Yes", when my insides were screaming, "No!" The wonderful thing about making that shift was that when I did give, I could do so with joy and was not weighing myself down with doing things my heart was not drawing me towards.

The more awake and aware I became, the more habits I found within myself that I wanted to shift. As I retrieved more and more of my daily energy by releasing my past and calming my mind, I had more energy available for making changes in other areas of my life. I kept following my intuition to the library for books to inspire further growth. Two books I came across began to focus my attention on developing new parenting habits, James Redfield's book, *The Celestine Prophecy*, and Wayne Dyer's book, *What Do You Really Want for Your Children*. I asked my soul for guidance on what parenting behaviors I needed to shift in order to allow my children to feel empowered and develop their own deep inner compass. My desire was for them to be able to actively develop their dreams and feel in their bellies that they had the personal power to create them in the world. I monitored my actions and worked diligently to release behaviors that did not promote that parenting goal.

One specific area that I chose to work on was to consciously see my children as already being the best possible expression of themselves and to hold that vision for them when they experienced times of self-doubt. It is difficult not to get pulled into an emotional meltdown that your child is experiencing, especially when they are highly charged at the time. I was very connected to my children and when they became fearful and emotionally worked up, their emotions triggered fears that also resided inside of me. As a result I would get drawn into their downward spiral. I consciously set an intention to release that behavior. I meditated and visualized staying inside myself and remaining calm in the face of their emotions. I saw myself holding my calmness and beaming it back to them, in an effort to "be" the stable ground supporting them.

I distinctly remember the first time I was able to do this for my daughter, Lindsey, when she was in the 7th grade. She was in the throes of changing hormones, feeling insecure and overwhelmed by the challenges facing her. As she sat in the middle of her bedroom floor sobbing, the intuitive voice inside me prompted me not to get drawn into her emotions. I sat down on the floor in front of her and calmly looked her directly in the eyes and said, "Lindsey, I have ultimate confidence in you and your abilities." I sat there for a moment without wavering, just looking her straight in the eyes with the clear intention of beaming my loving support to her. My response was so different from past behaviors that I think it took us both by surprise. I stayed sitting on the floor with her until the tears subsided and we calmly talked about her fears. I was struck with how my calm, reassuring energy seemed to wash over her.

Since a very young age, my son, David, had always been extremely hard on himself whenever he made a mistake. I actively worked with him to change the way he spoke to himself in his head. One day I sat him down after I heard him say, "I am the stupidest boy ever." He was probably about 6 years old at the time. I asked him, "Does Mommy talk to you like that?" He replied, "No". I said, "That's right, and you should never let anyone talk to you like that, including yourself. You don't deserve to be spoken to like that. We all make mistakes and do things we wish we hadn't done, but it's OK. We need to be gentle with ourselves." For several years I actively worked with him on changing the way he spoke to himself in his head. One day when David was 12 and Lindsey was about 16, Lindsey was very upset with herself over something. Overhearing the conversation, David walked into the room, looked at her and said, "You shouldn't talk to yourself like that. You should talk nice to yourself." I was stunned, and so proud of him!

Bliss

I become bliss
As I allow myself
To be an open
Conduit
for
Love

Gradually more and more jewelry booths began showing up at all of the local art fairs, as beading had caught on as a wonderful way to relax and create. As people stopped by my booth to gather ideas and inspiration to create their own pieces, I realized that I needed to branch out and do new things to keep my business thriving. I realized that over the past several years as I pursued my own inner healing, I was drawn to learn more to facilitate the emotional healing of others and use my own gift of sensitivity. I had met someone while I was doing my jewelry business that did massage work that felt so different from anything I had experienced before. She explained that she combined "energy" work with the massage. The after effects were very emotionally healing for me and I was intrigued to learn more. I tentatively signed up for a few classes at a massage school that had programs in all sorts of modalities. The first course I signed up for was an Ayurvedic warm oil massage called Abyanga. The class began on Friday evening and then lasted all day on Saturday and Sunday. When I arrived on Friday with my sheets and towels, the room was packed with students carrying their supplies, mostly young gals in their twenties. A bit of panic set in for me as I realized I was nearly twice their age! The teacher was a young man named Daniel, who had traveled from Los Angeles to teach the class. I learned that we would be completely nude for the massage with a sheet on top of us. First the left side of the body was exposed and massaged with warm herbal infused oil and then the right side. Next we turned over and repeated the massage on the front side of our bodies. I was to pair with a total stranger to do this! What had I gotten myself into? Talk about feeling vulnerable – I felt completely emotionally unprepared for this exposure, and it was all I could do not to run screaming from the room. I somehow made it through the first evening and actually returned the next morning at nine o'clock to begin again. The anxiety I was feeling brought all sorts of old emotional material to the surface and made it difficult at first to relax. I used my empathic ability to choose a massage partner that I trusted and tried to open myself to receive the experience. Of all the massage classes I have taken, this particular massage turned out to be the most nurturing and soothing massage I ever learned. The warm oil and long rhythmic strokes were very calming. By the end of the weekend I felt transformed by the experience and certain that again my passion was leading me in the right direction.

There were so many choices of modalities at the massage school and I knew so little, that I decided to go with the basic therapeutic massage emphasis. It seemed the obvious place to start and there would be opportunities to sample other "energy" modalities such as CranioSacral and Polarity. Each class presented a wealth of new experiences and opened me up to new concepts. My first instructors introduced me to the concept of "holding sacred space" for the client in a massage session. It is a conscious awareness that is cultivated as part of the massage process. This concept resonated deeply with me as an opportunity to relate to someone else as a unique piece of the divine whole. All judgment is suspended in that space and we hold the other as a sacred being. In that open space, we allow their physical, emotional and spiritual bodies to receive or release whatever is necessary for them to move towards wholeness and balance. The massage therapist becomes a conduit to facilitate this process.

I was born under the sign of Cancer, and true to my birth sign, one of my primary motivations has always been to nurture others. What I was learning at massage school took the concept of nurturing to an entirely new level. I was getting in touch with a deeper part of myself and experiencing what it was like to connect with someone else on that level. The concept of an exchange of "energy" between people was familiar to me, but up until that point, I had not consciously realized how much information I had been intuitively receiving in this way. Each of my teachers had their unique way of describing what took place during a massage, and how to keep yourself "grounded" as you initiated a massage session. I became more and more familiar with maintaining a deep inner connection to myself as I practiced various meditation and breathing techniques. In a massage session it is important to stay in tune with yourself so that you don't unconsciously take on the client's "energy".

As part of my electives I was able to take a few classes in the techniques that were more "energy" related. The first one I signed up for was CranioSacral therapy. The first night of class we practiced feeling the energy between our hands as we held them apart. It felt like an invisible balloon that actually held resistance to the pressure of our hands moving towards it. Even though I was open to this idea, I was actually surprised that I could really feel it and describe it. Next we were to pair up with someone and take turns lying on the massage table and sensing each other's energy field. Now I was getting nervous and my mind start racing with all kinds of doubts. How was I supposed to pair up with a complete stranger and without even touching them, just holding my hands out towards them, walk around their body and describe their energy field? My anxiety started rising and my inner chatter was running in circles. My partner wanted me to go first, and I reluctantly agreed, secretly thinking that I would probably just have to make up something to say. I stood a few feet from the massage table, and began to practice the techniques I had learned to get grounded and still inside. I reminded myself that I had actually felt the energy between my own hands and asked my mind to please shift from using words to simply "feeling". As I breathed deeply and slowly my anxiety dissipated. I held my hands up with palms toward my partner on the table, and began to slowly walk around her, staying about a foot from her body. Starting near her head, I thought I could actually feel her energy field and it felt strong. As I moved down her right side, her energy field felt pretty consistent. I began to tune into the pressure against my hands and almost felt like I could lean against it. As I rounded her feet and switched to her left side, the feeling changed so much, it took me by surprise. I realized how much I had been leaning into the energy, because all at once the pressure disappeared about midway up her calf and was totally gone by her knee! I summoned up my courage and said, "Has your knee been bothering you?" Her eyes got wide with disbelief as she told me that she had been practicing a martial art and doing a lot of kicking. She kicked with her right leg and kept falling on the left leg. As a consequence, her left knee was really sore and weak. I don't know who was more stunned, my partner or me! It was the beginning for me of learning to tune into the nonverbal information we are all receiving. The better I got at becoming still inside and anchoring myself into that stillness, the better I was at feeling the energy of others.

CranioSacral is a very gentle technique where the therapist assesses the rhythmic flow of craniosacral fluid from the head down to the base of the spine and assists the body in removing any obstacles to the natural flow of this system. The CranioSacral system is made up of all the bones in your skull, face and mouth, and is connected to the lower end of your spine via the fluid in your spinal column. Trauma to any part of the system, including the sacrum can interfere with the natural flow of this fluid, and can affect how your brain and spinal cord function.

At the final evening of the series of CranioSacral classes I received the most wonderful energetic release! My partner was doing a session for me, and about halfway through, as she held one hand underneath my sacrum and one hand on my belly my sacrum heated up and began to palpably pulse! She looked down at me with big round eyes, and said, "Do you feel that?" "YES!" I replied. She held her hands in position until the pulsing subsided and the heat began to diminish. We both knew that some energy had definitely been released! I woke the next morning with a strong pain in my lower back and could barely function. It was the 4th of July and we had planned on going to see fireworks, but I didn't think I could sit for long with the pain. I laid in bed most of the day, but was at peace about the pain, knowing that I had received a large energetic release the evening before, and my body was probably just shifting to accommodate the change. The pain diminished over the next few days. I realized that whatever had taken place had changed something in my lower pelvis, and I no longer had the chronic lower backache that I had had for years.

As I navigated my way through massage school, I continued to encounter people and situations that deepened my understanding of the inner healing work that can free up our energy to feel more joy and loving connectedness to our everyday life. The CranioSacral class had opened me up to trusting my instincts in feeling the energy of others, and also to the healing benefits of an energy session for myself. Some instructors were especially skilled at facilitating the learning, and I began to seek out more classes from the ones I resonated with. The CranioSacral teacher was one of those, and I signed up for a Polarity class that she taught. This modality involved a little more dialogue between the therapist and the client. It was a small class of eight, and we became very comfortable with each other. I had always had a rather persistent feeling of burning or heaviness in my lower right groin area and was beginning to sense that it reflected an energy blockage. One of the other students was a very experienced Polarity energy facilitator who was auditing the class. She was also currently working in the clinic at the school. I decided to book a session with her with the intention of releasing whatever blockage was there in my lower groin. As I meditated at home in the few weeks before the session, I began to see a picture in my minds' eye of the experience that caused the blockage. I had become accustomed to "seeing" and "feeling" things about other people as I did energy work for them, so I trusted that what my higher self was showing me about the nature of this energy blockage was real. The only odd part about it for me was that it was not from this lifetime. The event I kept visioning took place in the dimly lit corner of a medieval church at night. I was lying on the floor and over me was a priest who had a red-hot burning spear of metal in his hand. He was enraged with me because I had been actively promoting the idea that each of us has a personal connection to the divine, and we did not have to rely solely on the clergy to connect to Spirit. He was angry that my actions were eroding his power in the community, and decided that I needed to be dealt with. He killed me by plunging the burning metal rod into my lower right groin. When I went to the massage session, I described my insight to the therapist. I also briefly described my experience of having a baby at 19 and giving him up for adoption. I told her I had moved through the process of forgiving everyone involved, except for the doctor who seemed to be trying to teach me a lesson. The therapist combined CranioSacral and Polarity techniques in our session. She began to move her hands to release the blockage in my groin, and asked me to actively assist in energetically releasing it. It felt like anger that did not belong to me. As we worked in sync, I felt the burning in my groin flow out of me. At that instant I had a sudden flash of knowing that the priest who had killed me in that lifetime was the same person as the doctor who had delivered the son I had given up for adoption in this lifetime! I was a little taken aback, and before I could even get the words out, the therapist looked down at me and said, "I think the priest you have been visualizing was the same person as the doctor who delivered your son when you were 19!" I was a little unsettled, as I had never really had such a vivid past life memory, nor ever related one to a current life situation. Her observation was that it was interesting that he had tried to kill me in one lifetime by thrusting something into me, and then hurt me in this lifetime by harshly pulling something out of me. I was so grateful to the therapist and struck by the increased awareness that can be facilitated in an "energy" session like CranioSacral or Polarity.

My head was spinning as I left the massage clinic and drove home. I did not share my experience with anyone else. Instead I began to slowly digest it over the next several days. Was it possible that I could forgive this individual for actions that had caused me pain in this lifetime and death in another? Once again, I held the intention of forgiveness in my meditation practice and began to view him from a soul perspective. I meditated on what type of emotional wound causes people to hurt each other in this way. Issues of trying to control others arise from an internal feeling of being disconnected from our loving center. The more disconnected we feel, the more we try to lash out in anger or control others. I imagined a sacred open space with him sitting across from me. I allowed myself to feel his woundedness, and then to send him forgiveness for his actions towards me in both lifetimes. I allowed the anger inside me to melt and release, flowing out of me like a liquid. I had learned new meditation techniques in massage school, and one in particular felt very comfortable to me. I anchored myself to the earth by imagining a cord of energy going from the base of my spine deep into the earth. I also sent a cord of energy from the top of my head into the sky to connect to divine energy from above. This technique worked well in this situation, as I allowed the anger to release into the earth to be transmuted. What flowed into me was a feeling of regaining access to a part of myself that had been energetically cut off.

The final part of the process at massage school involved doing 50 hours of massage for customers in the school massage clinic. Each day I did a little meditation to prepare to hold sacred space for my clients. One day as I was entering the building, I heard a distinct inner voice say to me, "We are going to give you an experience today that you really need." Hmmm, I thought – I wonder what that means? I went in and put my things in my locker, same as every other day. I went to check my clients and found out that my second massage client was an "energy healer" that taught at the school. The clinic manager told me she gave him to me because she thought I would do a good job, based on the feedback customers had been giving the clinic about their experiences with me. I was very excited and thought to myself, "Wow, this will probably be an amazing experience!" My first client went very well, and I went out to greet my second client and walked him back to the massage room. His first request was that I turn off the music being piped into the room and get a CD player to play a special CD he brought of his own music. I went off to find a CD player, but there were none at the clinic. He then requested that I have them play his music CD to the entire clinic, if that was the only way he could hear it. I went off to make that request, and the clinic manager agreed to do it. Next he asked to close the door to the room, which we were instructed to leave slightly ajar, as we were student therapists. Now, I was beginning to feel uncomfortable, but I was afraid to say no to this respected person, so I agreed. Lastly, he asked if I could dim the lights, but as there was no control for this, he asked me to throw a towel over the light sconce on the wall. I reluctantly did it. About ten minutes into the massage, I could smell something burning, and just assumed he had lit some incense somewhere when I had left the room. I ignored it and carried on. The smell grew stronger, and he finally lifted his head and asked me what was burning. Oh my gosh! I looked up and saw that the towel I had thrown over the light sconce had almost caught fire! I quickly grabbed it off and stomped on it. By now, I was feeling very unsettled, and had to summon all my inner calm to keep my composure and continue for another 40 minutes with the massage. Partway through, I heard the music change, and found out later that a few clients had complained about the new music and they had switched it back to the regular music the clinic always played. Needless to say, it was not a wonderful experience. As I was redoing the sheets on the massage table afterwards, I reflected on the internal message I had received upon entering the clinic that day. I asked myself, "What did that experience teach me?" The answer was that I had done things I was uncomfortable with and allowed my personal boundaries to be breached, because I had allowed myself to feel less than equal to this other person. I had predetermined that because of his reputation it was more important to fulfill his requests than to follow my gut instincts. This can happen in any area of our life where we give our personal power to someone else and don't trust our own inner guidance. I thanked the Spirit for the experience and vowed to stay true to myself in all ways.

After completing massage school I pursued my own business as a massage therapist, traveling to my client's homes. I had been self employed for years with my jewelry business and reluctant to go to work for someone else. I had some wonderful experiences, but was not completely sure what direction I wanted to take my business in, as I was still wanting to learn more of the energy techniques I had touched upon in school. I decided to set it aside for a while and go back to work in an office in order to help provide a regular income and health insurance for our family. My husband and I were both self-employed and the cost of our family health insurance was rising dramatically each year. Our daughter, Lindsey, was now in college and we wanted to be able to fully pay her expenses so she could focus on her studies. I felt it would only be for a few years until both our kids were out of college and I could go back to developing a new business venture combining my artistic creativity with my desire to assist others with emotional healing.

Sonoran Twilight

Sunlight is waning,
The air grows moist and heavy.
I drink in the sweet nectar
Of desert blossoms
With slow, deep breaths.
As my awareness expands
And merges with their scent
I am transformed.
For a timeless moment
I am one
With their essence.

T he more I became attuned to my inner self, the more aware I became of how various people, situations or environments either strengthened my energy or depleted it. I set an inward intention to move toward experiences that supported my inner peace. As a consequence, this also involved moving away from or letting go of activities that did not strengthen my inner core. I found myself being drawn more and more to spend time outdoors, either hiking the local mountain preserves or just meditating in my own backyard. I found something truly healing about immersing myself in the natural beauty around me and I began to crave it on a regular basis.

My husband and I had begun to take regular neighborhood walks, which we both found relaxing and stimulating at the same time. Walking outdoors together became an opportunity to share our daily experiences as well as discuss concerns about our two children. After several months of regular walks, we both noticed that being outside in the fresh air and moving as we talked improved the energy flow between us and facilitated new ways of working together. We expanded on the walks by trying various hikes on local hiking trails and found an area that we both loved in the Dreamy Draw Mountain preserve, about 15 minutes from our home. In that beautiful desert preserve, surrounded by blooming cacti, singing birds, and lizards darting across our path, we both felt renewed and energized. We found one trail that became our favorite, with a fairly good climb that got our hearts pumping and ended in an outcropping of exposed white snowy quartz. There were huge boulders of the white quartz that we would sit and rest on, soaking up the Arizona sunshine. Over time this sanctuary of white quartz boulders became a place where we would share intimate emotions. We laughed and cried there together, always leaving with a renewed sense of connectedness. Jim and I came to view this place as a "power place" for us, where our energy was renewed and rejuvenated. It made total sense to me, as I knew from my jewelry making and studying the energy of gemstones that quartz is the most powerful energy amplifier on the planet. We each had our favorite white snowy quartz boulder to rest on. From that high vantage point in the preserve, we could see for miles over the northeast part of the city. Sometimes we would just sit in silence, breathing deeply, soaking in the beauty of the view. One of my favorite things to do was pinch off a tiny sprig of one of the creosote bushes nearby and rub its sticky leaves between my fingertips. It was like aromatherapy for me as I held it up to my nose, and drank in the scent. I knew that this was a potent plant and its active ingredients have been used for medicinal purposes. For me breathing in its rich scent was uplifting and invigorating.

As the weather grew hot in Phoenix and it became more and more difficult to hike locally during the day, we ventured out of town to hike in the cooler areas of Arizona. We just searched on Google for "hiking trails in Arizona", and found lots of specific trail information shared by individuals and groups. We were attracted to Prescott, which is just about an hour and a half northwest of Phoenix. We tried a few trails and found one that we loved called the Groom Creek Trail on a mountain just outside Prescott. The trail was a giant circle in the forest that was 9 miles long. We would always head in the same direction towards the ranger station lookout tower at the far side of the circular trail, hiking in as far as our schedule would allow. Each time we would make it a little further on the trail towards the lookout tower, but never reached it. Finally one Saturday we totally cleared our schedule so that we had no deadline for being home, and vowed to make it to the lookout tower. Wow! What an incredible 360 degree view there was from that vantage point. Pine forest stretched like a blanket of green in every direction. We sat soaking up the view eating sandwiches we had carried along.

Each time we hiked that Groom Creek Trail we encountered something we hadn't seen before. One time there was a hawk and a big black crow that held a lengthy conversation in the trees above us. This struck me as a beautiful metaphor for my husband and I, as he loves hawks and I love black crows. Another time pairs of large tarantula spiders crossed our path twice, heading in the same direction. We jokingly decided that they must have been heading to the same celebration at some remote forest location.

The walking and hiking were very beneficial for my husband and I together, but I also found I enjoyed doing my meditation alone outside. The more I meditated outside the more I wanted to create a sacred oasis in my own backyard. I had always enjoyed planting shrubs and flowers and enjoying their beauty in our yard, but I wanted something that I could have more of a daily relationship with. We had a long, narrow side yard that was just landscaped with gravel and I decided to create my space there with a vegetable and herb garden. The more I deepened my connection within, the more everyday tasks, such as creating a garden became opportunities to see metaphors about spiritual growth. First there is the process of clearing the old wounds (gravel) to reveal the beautiful core (ground) underneath. I began to nourish the dense clay dessert ground with something called fish emulsion to make it more fertile for supporting plants. We jokingly referred to it as "fish pooh water" at our house, because it had a rather pungent odor. I had decided to nurture the ground slowly and naturally, so the first year I used nothing but fish emulsion and organic fertilizer. I planted small root vegetables such as radishes, carrots and scallions to begin loosening up the soil. I also planted a grapevine and created a trellis so that the vine would grow across the top of the garden to shade it from the harsh sun in the summer heat.

The garden became a tangible way for me to connect daily with the energy and rhythms of nature. Sometimes it was just for a few minutes to admire the new leaves unfurling on a broccoli plant or the buds opening on the dormant grapevine as it reawakened after winter. Other times it became my morning meditation spot and I sat cross-legged on the ground at the edge of it, letting the calmness of the grapevine canopy envelope me as I meditated. I found that doing this first thing in the morning, before I headed off to work helped me anchor to the stillness within me. It became easier during the day to mentally bring myself back to that physical feeling of calm. Feelings of bliss and contentment would wash over me as I sat and practiced deep breathing to fill my solar plexus with the energy. I would imagine a loving ball of light glowing within my belly and would sit breathing deeply as it expanded inside me. When the environment at work grew chaotic, I would mentally come back inside myself and ground myself back into that deep calmness.

As I connected more deeply with the earth I began to incorporate more daily practices to honor her. As a family we enjoyed the connection of eating vegetables and fruit directly from our garden. The next natural step was to begin composting so that we could complete the circle and give back to the richness of the soil. I started simply with a cardboard box near the garden. Everything went in there.... scraps of leftover food from a meal, the discarded vegetable trimmings from my cutting board, coffee grounds, banana peels, egg shells, dryer lint, dry leaves, grass clippings, paper from the shredder....basically everything but meat was tossed inside. It became a mindfulness practice, as we were consciously returning organic material to the earth on a daily basis. I watered and stirred the compost pile a few times a week and was captivated by the transformation. Basically we were creating a lovely meal for the bugs, which happily decomposed our discarded items and in turn gave us rich, dark dirt to fertilize our garden with. About three months into the composting I started a second pile, this time in a large plastic storage box that I purchased from Target. I drilled several dozen quarter inch holes in the bottom for drainage and began a fresh pile. I allowed the initial pile to finish decomposing for two more months until it resembled dark brown dirt, and then spread it over the surface of our garden. Reflecting on the process I saw how it mirrored our own inner emotional work. The entire journey of our life is a series of experiences and when lived with awareness can become a rich compost pile to fertilize future growth in us.

The Gem

My silent witness
Observes myself
As a many faceted gem
And extends
Unconditional Love
To both the
Dark and the Light.

Although I had cleared the emotional wounds that had the largest impact on my life, I realized I could continue to benefit by doing additional emotional clearing work on myself. I consciously did a life review, working backwards to see if there were any other areas where I had become emotionally stuck. When a particular person or circumstance came to mind, I would allow myself the opportunity to do a focused meditation on forgiving whoever was involved. In these meditations I would mentally invite the person to enter into a sacred space with me. I would visualize them sitting across from me and consciously open my heart to them. If the emotional wound I had received from the experience was deep, it would sometimes take several sessions before I could hold them with compassion, forgive them and send them unconditional love. I entered into these sessions with a deep knowing that others only act in ways that wound us out of their own sense of separateness. Once I felt my heart energy flowing in forgiveness, I would visualize a loving energy repairing the emotional wound inside me. It was as if whatever part of me had been damaged from the experience was now reconnected to my true self and available for me to access. As I regained access to more and more of my authentic self, it became easier for me to keep a healthy emotional balance from a perspective of self-reference, instead of relying on the opinions of others. Clearing my personal emotional history allowed me to more fully experience all of the love and joy present in my life.

I maintain a practice that whenever my emotional "buttons" get pushed, I take a moment afterwards to stop and ask myself what I am still carrying around that is no longer serving me. Daily I set the intention that I am releasing anything that is blocking my soul from its highest expression of itself. It has been my experience that whenever I focus my attention consistently on something, whether positive or negative, its effect does increase in my life. This has made me very conscious of what I am allowing my thoughts to focus on every day. When I start feeling stuck in life, it is a signal that I have allowed my mental activity to fall back into old habits.

In order to surround myself with reminders of what my soul chooses to experience, I wrote seven poems as daily reminders. I copied the poems on small note cards and set them on my bathroom counter so that I would see them first thing each morning. I kept the poems in the same order, so that a particular poem falls on the same day each week. After several years, this practice established a certain spiritual rhythm to my week. Each week I endeavor to sink a little deeper into the feeling of each poem, as I move to fully open my heart to embrace life.

The poem for Monday reminds me that it is important to move towards what we feel passionate about in life, as that is how the soul communicates with us. Those inspired feelings that stir us from within are the soul's way of drawing us towards fulfilling our life's purpose. When we entice our ego to step aside and perceive life from our soul's perspective, we truly do see the divine in everything.

> *The soul yearns to express*
> *Its unique gift*
> *As it aligns with the*
> *Pulse of the universe*
> *As our passion is ignited*
> *And the ego steps aside*
> *We reflect back to others*
> *The radiant light*
> *Of all living beings*

Tuesday's poem keeps me focused on seeing the divine in every person I come into contact with, even when they do not see it in themselves.

> *I hold sacred space*
> *For the*
> *Divine spark*
> *To emerge*
> *In every person*
> *I come into*
> *Contact*
> *With*
> *Today*

Wednesday's poem is an expression of the positive benefits of a regular practice of meditation. The more I meditate, the deeper the feeling of inner peace and the stronger my intuitive voice becomes.

> *As our attention floats*
> *In the stream of silence*
> *Spontaneous knowing*
> *Bubbles up*
> *From within us*
> *And with its flow*
> *Brings truth and bliss*

Thursday's poem reminds me that the Loving Source of the universe is supporting the desires of my soul, and orchestrating the fulfillment of my intentions. This is all occurring while I surrender control and embrace the natural flow of life.

> *As a pebble*
> *Ripples across*
> *The surface of a pond*
> *My intentions shoot out*
> *And skim across the universe*
> *With the*
> *Power*
> *To create*
> *My dreams*

Friday's poem reflects the deep stillness that we each have the ability to connect with. As we go inside ourselves in meditation and reside in this awareness, we have access to a nonphysical place where miracles occur.

As I go deep within
I touch the space
Where my soul
Bathes in infinite bliss
From that space
I can manifest
My deepest intention

Saturday's poem is a reminder that we already possess everything we need to fulfill our soul's purpose as long as we consciously move towards embodying the awareness that will draw it forth.

The creative fire within me
Draws forth
All the necessary attributes
To allow my soul
To fully
Express
Itself

For Sunday, I chose a reminder that we are immersed in divine, loving assistance.

Each day is a cosmic dance
Where the playful voice
Of our divine partner
Speaks to us
In every moment
We are truly present

Nimbus

Laying on a blanket
Of soft, moist grass
My spirit soars upward
And merges with the clouds,
Surrendering control,
Shifting shape,
Allowing myself access
To the field of
Infinite
Possibilities.

Although I was not actively practicing as a massage therapist, I wanted to make sure I kept my license current. I knew that I would pursue it again, once I had the time to go back to school and study some of the energy techniques I was drawn to. One of the classes I took to fulfill my continuing education credits was a Hypno-Meditation Self Care class at a place called Healing Arts Connection. Marsha Craven, who ran Healing Arts Connection had a strong reputation as a gifted CranioSacral therapist. I was really looking forward to the four evenings of quiet meditation spent in the company of other like-minded people. I had noticed in massage school that there was definitely a deepening effect to any massage or meditation experience when there was a room full of other individuals who were also earnestly seeking to open their hearts and gain greater self-awareness. Each evening of the class was to have a different focus: Self-Healing, Abundance/Prosperity, Soul Journeys and Past Life Re-call. I thoroughly enjoyed each evening and received some wonderful insights from each of the meditations.

The one evening that really stood out for me was the Past Life Re-call meditation. Marsha led us through several different past life re-call sessions and had us write down as much information as we could remember after each one before continuing on, including whether there were any persons in that life that we knew now. I had two different sessions that were very graphic and full of details. In one I was a Native American woman and was living in an elevated adobe structure that overlooked a valley with a desert terrain. I lived with my sister and we were both pottery artists. We dug the clay for our pottery from the ground and painted intricate designs on the finished pieces. It was in the late 1700's. I felt very close to my sister. We shared a lot of humor and thoroughly enjoyed being together. I had the realization that my sister in that lifetime was my son, David, in this lifetime. Our relationship in this lifetime has the same qualities of warmth and humor. We have always been very emotionally close. When he was young I used to think that he could literally read my mind, as he was so intuitive about how I was feeling.

The second past life re-call that was memorable was one where I was a dark skinned male living in a jungle area somewhere on the African coast near the ocean. My younger brother in that lifetime was my father in this lifetime. We were very dedicated to each other as brothers, and I had the feeling that neither of us had married or had a family. It had been a very playful, carefree life full of joy. We were elderly and in our culture it was acceptable to choose when you felt you had lived a full life and were ready to die. In my re-call I was choosing to go into the jungle and allow my spirit to depart, and my younger brother was very sad that I was choosing to go, because he would miss me so much. This memory also seemed to mirror the feeling of closeness I have to my father in this lifetime, especially when I was young and still living at home. I always felt a bit protective of him when I was in my early teens, as his emotional needs seemed to get overlooked in our large family.

With each new experience I was having, I was continually in awe of our human ability to access deep information about ourselves simply by setting a conscious intention and holding it in our awareness. The experiences necessary to fulfill that intention are drawn to us by a creative, loving force that is nothing short of miraculous. I was also gaining a great respect for the power of meditation to quiet the mind and give us access to the nonphysical part of reality and the more subtle energies of life. Another metaphor related to my gardening came to mind. I noticed that when I first planted a perennial plant such as a red pepper plant, most of the growth occurred beneath the surface as the roots were becoming established. Once this occurred, the visible part of the plant expanded, as the roots were gathering sufficient nutrients to support the growth. I thought of my meditation practice as my roots, and the more often I meditated the deeper they sank into the Loving Source within me. In turn this connection fostered the opening of my heart and my ability to live from that deep heart space.

Grace

Grace nourishes
My heart center to
Open
and
Receive

I am fortunate enough to live in the same city as most of my extended family. As my parents aged they each had their own minor health issues. In her early seventies my mom developed an intestinal blockage and had to have part of her colon removed. There was no cancer involved, but the surgery left her with some physical challenges that were a daily struggle for her. She wrestled with keeping up her enthusiasm for life as these physical issues sometimes limited her ability to be as mobile as she wanted to be. My mom was such an intelligent and well-read woman. She never had the opportunity to attend college and make the kind of professional contribution that she was so capable of, but often came up with profound insights from her zest for reading and digesting a wide array of topics. It was difficult to see her getting discouraged by the physical challenges after that surgery. I found myself thinking of her often, sending the prayer that in her next life she would be born into a situation where she might have all the opportunities to cultivate her many talents and gain the recognition of her keen intellect that she desired. Then in the late spring of 2008, she was diagnosed with small cell lung cancer. In the weeks before the diagnosis, she had been struggling with insomnia and some sinus issues, so by the time the doctors realized that the underlying issue was lung cancer, she was feeling pretty weak.

Our large family rallied around her and my dad to provide both physical and emotional support. Over the next 7 months, my mom basically never left her house again, except to go to the doctor or a chemo appointment. We cooked, cleaned, gave back massages, and accompanied them to her chemo appointments. After several rounds of chemo, she gained some strength and appeared to be getting back to feeling like her normal self. Unfortunately, it was short lived as the cancer cells that were still left were resistant to the chemo. She grew weaker again, barely able to walk to the kitchen table to eat. We had to sit her on a chair in the shower to bathe her. The first time I helped her onto the chair in the shower, I was struck with what a blessing it was to be able to take care of her in this tender way. She was vulnerable as a child, dependent on others for her every need.

Eventually my mom was exhausted from the ordeal of chemo and expressed her strong desire to be allowed to stay at home and end the treatments. She wanted to be in control of the few choices she had left to make. We contacted hospice and in their wonderful care, began the last several weeks of her life. I had one sibling who lived out of town, my older sister, Kathy. She had been coming every three weeks or so during my mom's illness, and she flew out to be with us once again.

While caring for my mom during her illness, a strong desire arose in me to make sure I was physically present for her when she transitioned. I expressed it to my brother John to make sure someone else was aware of my inner commitment to be physically with her as her spirit departed. It was during this time that I went for a massage at the massage school where I had taken classes. I was fortunate enough to get a therapist who I had known from classes and knew him to be a very compassionate, spiritual person. We engaged in conversation during the massage, but near the end of the hour when he was working on my scalp, the conversation ceased and I sank deeply into the relaxation. A scene appeared in my inner vision from a previous lifetime with my mother. We were Native Americans living in a wooded area. I was a young male walking with a group of men through a path in the trees, just arriving home from a spiritual journey. As we emerged from the forest we arrived in our village. People were gathered around a body, which had been wrapped and bound to a stretcher in preparation for a funeral. I realized in an instant that it was my mom from this life. We had a significant relationship during that lifetime and she had passed away when I was away. The community was waiting for our return to do the funeral ceremony for her. The awareness also came to me that she had sadness in her heart when she passed, as she had wanted me to be with her as her spirit departed. Just as I was feeling the sadness of that experience, I felt myself whisked away from the scene and now was soaring over a large body of water. The message was that I was shown this not to relive the sadness, but to understand my current life desire to make sure I was physically by my mom's side as she departed. A deep sense of peace washed over me, as I knew I would be able to keep my commitment to her this time, and possibly heal an old wound for her in the process. The healing part for me was that this memory shed a lot of light on the personal dynamics of my relationship with my mom during this lifetime.

We began hospice care for my mom at home and were grateful to find that their staff was so compassionate and willing to offer advice. After a few short weeks, my mom asked hospice if a nurse could please stay 24 hours a day from then on. A hospital bed was delivered the next morning. Although we did not realize it, she must have known she would be passing in just a few days. She grew very agitated over the next two days and wanted at least one of us family members to be sitting holding her hand the entire time, even through the night. We coordinated our times and made sure we were there for her. On Sunday I spent almost the entire day sitting with her, watching her favorite CSI shows on TV. On Monday morning, I received a call at work that she was not responsive, and had been in a deep sleep all night. One by one, as phone calls were made, all six of her children arrived and with my dad gathered around her bed. We held her hands, stroked her head and tearfully told her what a wonderful mom she had been and how much we were going to miss her. Her breathing became slower and shallower and then eventually she drew her last small breath. The hospice nurse told us that it was the most peaceful death she had ever witnessed.

Several months after my mom passed away I signed up for a series of Reiki classes taught by the same wonderful woman, Marsha Craven, who I had taken the meditation class from. I was really looking forward to the experience, as these classes attracted like-minded people who were also interested in spiritual growth and healing. The first two sessions of Reiki were offered on a Tuesday and Wednesday, and the third class was several weeks later on a Saturday. I was grateful to have a job that offered the flexibility of taking time off, and looked forward to spending two weekdays in peaceful bliss surrounded by fellow seekers. The experiences I had surpassed all my expectations.

Marsha began the first day explaining the history of Reiki as a healing modality encompassing spirit, energy and matter. She went on to outline the teaching lineage through which she had learned Reiki, tracing directly back to Mikao Usui. As always, she was compassionate, humble, and full of humor as she spoke in her wonderful thick southern accent. She explained that as part of our training, we would each receive three Reiki attunements, one each day of class. Shortly before lunch on the first day, we prepared for our first Reiki attunement. Marsha had two assistants who would be doing one part of the individual attunement, while she did the other part. We each set our personal intentions, as Marsha invoked the assistance of our heavenly Mother/Father as well as all our guides and teachers to energetically assist in the attunements. Beautiful music played in the background as we sat on chairs with our eyes closed and hands folded in front of us, as in prayer.

A deep sense of peace enveloped the room as Marsha and her assistants moved quietly, doing the individual attunements. I just remember feeling very relaxed as the first attunement was done with quiet hand movements around my head and hands. As the second person set their hands gently on my shoulders, I instantly began to weep uncontrollably. My eyes were closed and tears streamed down my cheeks. The physical sensation that accompanied it was as if a sheath of liquid was pouring off my body around my midsection and melting away. I sensed a deep emotion that seemed several lifetimes old of intense sadness at how unkind human beings can choose to be to one another on this planet. It felt distinctly like my mom and she instantly came to mind, as if I were shedding some deep emotion she had been carrying around all her life. When the attunements were complete, and we all opened our eyes, I sat quietly trying to compose myself. Marsha asked for people to share their experience, and several people spoke. Too moved to talk about what I had felt, I sat quietly taking it all in.

The day progressed and we picked partners to practice on. We each took turns doing an hour-long session on the massage tables. By the end of the eight-hour day warmth and camaraderie filled the room. I left feeling extremely relaxed and peaceful. The next day as I walked into the room, Barbara, one of Marsha's assistants, greeted me. She had been so warm and open the day before that I felt compelled to share my experience during the attunement the day before. She urged me to share it with the group that day.

At the end of the morning's instruction, we prepared to receive our second Reiki attunement, sitting as we did the day before, with hands folded as in prayer. Again, Marsha invoked the assistance of our heavenly Mother/Father and all of our guides and teachers to assist us. A deep feeling of peace filled the space as the attunements began. I felt Marsha lay her hands gently on my shoulders, and again began instantly to weep. In my mind's eye, a scene appeared. I was back in the lifetime I had remembered several months earlier, when my mom and I had been Native Americans and she had passed away while I was gone from the village. It was dark and I was standing in a circle of people. In the center of the circle a huge fire was burning. I looked over at the opposite side of the circle and saw an older, broad shouldered man that I recognized as my shaman mentor during that lifetime. I was leading the funeral ceremony for my mom in that lifetime, after we had returned from our spiritual quest and found she had passed. As I stood there taking in the scene, my mom from my current life came and tapped me on the shoulder and forgave me for not having been present for her when she passed during that life. The tears were streaming uncontrollably down my cheeks now, as her forgiveness melted something inside me. The scene disappeared and again I sat quietly, struggling to gain my composure so that I could share my experiences with the group.

Others in the class began to share what they had felt during the attunement. I summoned up my courage and explained my experiences both from that attunement, as well as the one the day before. Her eyes full of compassion, Marsha said that my mom had still been in my "emotional body" after her passing, but that she saw her walk away from me the day before, when I had felt the melting feeling of liquid leaving my body. She said that as my mom walked away, she turned one last time to look at me. By forgiving me for that past life hurt, she had paved the way for a very deep healing for me. During the next two or three days I had several more recollections from that previous lifetime. It was as if a doorway had opened for a brief bit that allowed me to glimpse inside that lifetime. I remembered that my mentor's name was Raven, and that I had followed him around as a small child, climbing on his broad back as he sat preparing healing mixtures. My curiosity was so intense that he called me his "Little Bird" and eventually took me on as his apprentice. The memories brought feelings of joy and contentment.

Two weeks later I returned for the third Reiki class. At the end of the morning's instructions, Marsha prepared us to receive our third attunement. As the beautiful background music played, we all closed our eyes and opened our hearts. Marsha and her assistants moved among us, performing each individual attunement. When Marsha began my attunement, again a scene opened in my mind's eye and I could see my guides and angels standing around me, giving their blessing. It felt like a moment of completion for a spiritual journey I had begun lifetimes ago. I was filled with bliss and gratitude at all the loving support surrounding me.

The Reiki attunements healed something deep inside me and over the next several months, I found myself experiencing a great sense of peace. It also reignited my artistic nature. I developed a new business name and logo that came directly from those experiences – Twilight Crow Studio. I wasn't quite sure yet what type of creative work was coming next for me, but knew it would have something to do with assisting others on their healing paths.

I had been having issues with neck pain the week of the third Reiki class and decided to schedule a CranioSacral session with Marsha to see if she could release whatever was bothering me. By the time I went to see her, the pain felt like a muscle spasm and was quite intense at times. I checked in with myself to see if it was related to something my body was energetically trying to release. In my mind's eye I kept seeing myself in a setting from the Middle Ages in Europe. It was broad daylight and I was in a room hanging from a noose attached to the ceiling dying, after having been brutally raped. Several men were sitting around on stools, laughing and talking as I died. People on the walkway outside glanced in the open doorway as they walked by, but no one stopped.

Again it was a lifetime where I had been too open about my views and had been killed because of it. I had been the local herbal healer and men did not appreciate the knowledge I empowered the women with. I briefly described it to Marsha as the session began and told her I felt my neck pain was related to that past life death. She concurred and said she could "see" that I had died from trauma to my neck in several other lifetimes as well. The session went well and I left with some relief from the pain. It took several more days for the discomfort to wind its way out of my body. Again I meditated on forgiving the individuals in that past life who had hurt and killed me. I saw that as a result of being killed many times for my views, it was hard for me to step forward in this current lifetime and be open about my abilities and spiritual perspective. I was however filled with a sense of peace that I had finally healed enough of my past to move forward with more courage in this current lifetime.

Unfolding

Inside each of you
is an exquisite bud
waiting patiently
in blissful anticipation
to spring open
and display all of its
beauty, joy and magic

When we truly connect
to our inner wisdom
the bud unfolds
in all its splendor

During those months of insomnia years ago after Valerie passed away, I never would have imagined that I would be feeling as grounded and embraced by love as I do today. This is the gift waiting for each of you. Spirit is waiting for you in the silence within. This connection is not just for a select few. It is your birthright as a human being. You have all the answers you need right inside of you. As you peel back the inner layers and heal your emotional wounds, you will shed the false beliefs about yourself. What flows into that space instead is a deep peace and a feeling of being part of the Loving Source.

One truth that I have come to embrace is that if we consciously stay connected to our internal source, we can see the divine beauty in each person we come into contact with, even when they don't see it in themselves. We can "hold space" for them to step into the awareness that we are all connected not only to each other, but to the Loving Source. I work daily to consciously remind myself that people who are angry and hostile still possess the divine spark within them, but are simply feeling disconnected from the Loving Source of Spirit. This awareness allows me the flexibility not to take their anger personally, and at the same time to hold compassion for them in their feeling of separateness.

To keep my life moving forward in the direction of my dreams, I focus on being very honest with myself about what I need to keep myself in balance. I stay tuned in to my internal rhythms and make space for the types of meditation, food, exercise and creative activities that feed my soul. The more I am able to remain present in each moment, the easier life flows. When challenges show up, I look at them from a soul perspective and ask myself why I attracted the experience. The more I trust in my intuition, the deeper the connection grows. Feelings of gratefulness and joy arrive in a steady stream, as I feel more and more connected to the presence of love in everything.

For several years I have been keeping a journal in my computer with short notes on insights I have gained. Periodically I would review it to remind myself of how far I had already traveled on my journey, or to write a new piece of wisdom or bit of poetry. On December 31, 2009, I was meditating on my personal direction for the beginning of 2010 and was drawn to invest my creative energy in two things. The first was to do a cleanse diet, and the second was to write about my personal journey in the form of a book. I share my own inner journey in the hopes that something in my experience might inspire others to begin or continue their own inner healing. We are living in a very stressful time of human evolution, yet there is so much support available for our personal spiritual growth and healing. We are surrounded by amazing and insightful authors, speakers, artists and musicians who share their beautiful visions of human potential. We are just beginning to tap the potential of energy healing techniques such as Reiki and CranioSacral as they become more widely available and accepted in the mainstream of society. We are remembering that we need to honor this exquisite garden of a planet that is our home.

As children, we all feel boundless energy and enthusiasm for life. We feel the possibilities are endless. As we mature, we take on the limited thinking of our culture, and we slowly replace our own internal truth with the prevailing thinking of the time. As this happens, our connection to our true limitless self begins to whither, as we no longer feed and nourish the connection with our attention. It does not die, however, it simply lies in wait for the time we will again cultivate our inner ground and water it by trusting our own truth. The key to tapping into this boundless reservoir is to clear the inner pathways by healing our emotional wounds. By doing this we can truly live "in the moment" and experience the divine love that is within and all around us. As more and more people begin to live from this deep heart space, our earthly meadow will be awash in flowers.

About the Author

Mo Brady is an artist and Reiki Master living in Phoenix, Arizona with her two children, Lindsey and David. After receiving her BFA at Arizona State University, Mo pursued clothing and textile design in New York City. Learning papermaking from a studio in Soho, she began creating and selling sculptural handmade paper pieces in galleries in New York and Arizona. Drawn back to the beauty and serenity of the southwest desert she and her husband, Jim, moved back to Arizona in 1989. Her artistic pursuits continued to evolve to include working with gemstone energy in jewelry. After studying massage therapy and Reiki, she now combines her artistic pursuits with her desire to inspire and encourage others on their path of self-awareness.

In March of 2011 her husband, Jim, passed away from cancer. She was at his side and holding his hand as he took his last breath. Mo still feels his heartful presence and loving encouragement.

Many blessings to each of you on your own journey!